Twelve Sweet Months

Seasonal Anthems for equal or mixed voices & organ

Colin Mawby

Kevin Mayhew

We hope you enjoy *Twelve Sweet Months*. Further copies are
available from your local music shop or Christian bookshop.

In case of difficulty, please contact the publisher direct by writing to:

The Sales Department
KEVIN MAYHEW LTD
Rattlesden
Bury St Edmunds
Suffolk
IP30 0SZ

Phone 0449 737978
Fax 0449 737834

Please ask for our complete catalogue of outstanding Church Music.

First published in Great Britain in 1994 by Kevin Mayhew Ltd

© Copyright 1994 Kevin Mayhew Ltd

ISBN 0 86209 485 2

The music and texts in this book are protected by copyright and may not be reproduced
in any way for sale or private use without the consent of the copyright owner.

Front Cover: *April* (detail) from MS 39, Keble College, Oxford.
Reproduced by kind permission of Woodmansterne Picture Library.

Cover designed by Juliette Clarke and Graham Johnstone
Picture Research: Jane Rayson

Music Editor: Joanne Clarke
Music setting by Kevin Whomes

Printed and bound in Great Britain

Contents

	Page
Behold a simple tender babe (Christmas)	8
God is ascended (Ascension)	30
Have mercy on me, O God (Passiontide)	22
How amiable are thy dwellings (Patronal Festival)	60
I heard a great voice (All Saints)	54
O help us, Lord (Lent)	18
O praise the Lord, all ye nations (Easter)	25
O the depth of the riches (Trinity)	44
Pleasure it is (Harvest Festival)	48
Praise ye the Lord (Whitsun)	36
The shepherd (Advent)	4
The star which they saw in the East (Epiphany)	13

Composer's Note

I have tried to make *Twelve Sweet Months* as widely usable as possible and I hope they will be particularly useful for small choirs, especially those which do not have men, or are somewhat short of them. The upper parts are suitable for either ladies, girls or boys or a mixture of all three. The anthems, which cover the seasons of the Church's year may be sung in any one of the following ways: (a) in unison; (b) in two parts SA; or (c) exactly as written SA Men. If the singing is in unison or two parts the footnotes in the Christmas and Harvest Festival anthems should be followed carefully.

COLIN MAWBY

Other works by Colin Mawby published by Kevin Mayhew Ltd.

Organ Music: *Fanfares and Finales, Mood Music, Quiet Time Music* and *Gregorian Calendar*.

Choral Music: *Communion Songs, Festival Mass, In Memory of Me, Invocation 1, Invocation 2, Mass of the Holy City, Songs for Many Seasons* and *The Heavenly Christmas Tree*.

ADVENT

The Shepherd

Text: William Blake (1757-1827)
Music: Colin Mawby (*b.*1936)

© Copyright 1994 by Kevin Mayhew Ltd.
It is illegal to photocopy music.

CHRISTMAS

Behold a simple tender Babe

Text: Robert Southwell (1561-1595)
Music: Colin Mawby

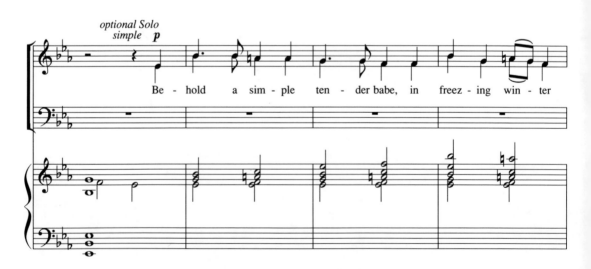

© Copyright 1994 by Kevin Mayhew Ltd.
It is illegal to photocopy music.

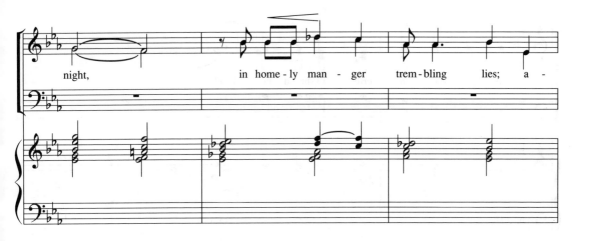

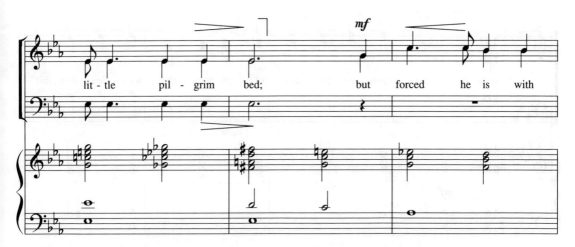

* ⌐ These bars should only be sung by the Sopranos and Altos in the absence of Men's voices.
  If men are present, the upper parts should be silent.

* ⌐ These bars should only be sung by the Sopranos if both Altos and Men are absent.

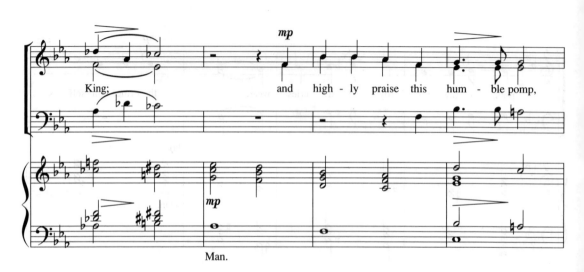
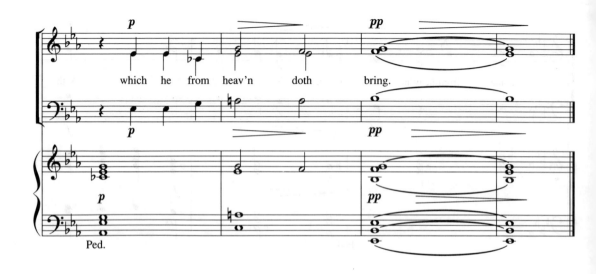

Epiphany

The Star which they saw in the East

Text: Matthew 2: 9-11
Music: Colin Mawby

© Copyright 1994 by Kevin Mayhew Ltd.
It is illegal to photocopy music.

LENT

O help us, Lord

Text: H. H. Milman (1791-1868)
Music: Colin Mawby

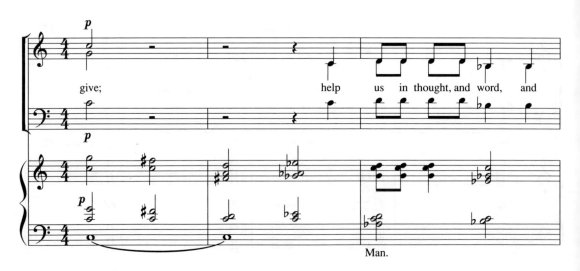

PASSIONTIDE

Have mercy on me, O God

Text: Psalms 51, 86
Music: Colin Mawby

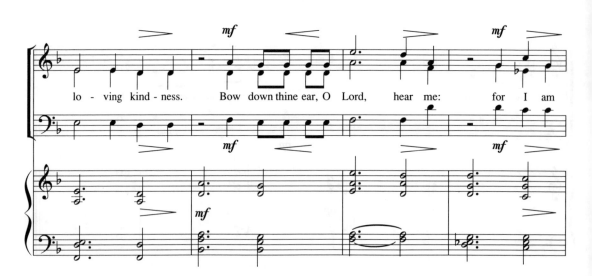

© Copyright 1994 by Kevin Mayhew Ltd.
It is illegal to photocopy music.

EASTER

O praise the Lord, all ye nations

Text: Psalm 117
Music: Colin Mawby

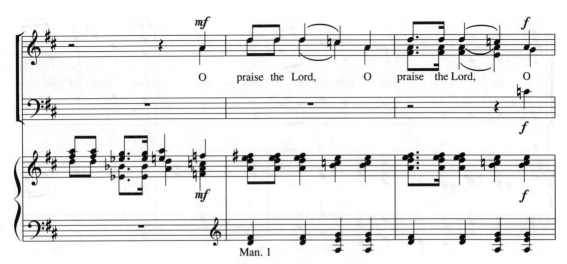

© Copyright 1994 Kevin Mayhew Ltd.
It is illegal to photocopy music.

ASCENSION

God is ascended

Text: Henry More (1614-1687)
Music: Colin Mawby

© Copyright 1994 by Kevin Mayhew Ltd.
It is illegal to photocopy music.

WHITSUN

Praise ye the Lord

Text: Psalm 150
Music: Colin Mawby

© Copyright 1994 by Kevin Mayhew Ltd.
It is illegal to photocopy music.

TRINITY

O the depth of the riches

Text: Romans 11: 33, 34, 36
Music: Colin Mawby

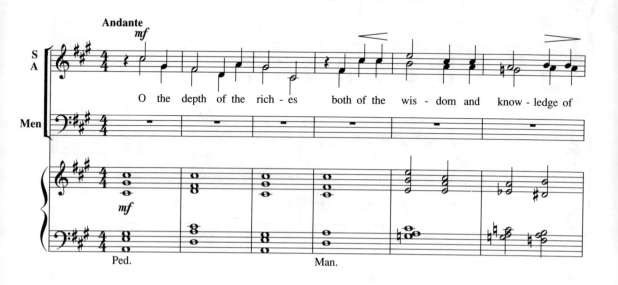

© Copyright 1994 by Kevin Mayhew Ltd.
It is illegal to photocopy music.

Harvest Festival

Pleasure it is

Text: William Cornish (*d.*1523)
Music: Colin Mawby

© Copyright 1994 by Kevin Mayhew Ltd.
It is illegal to photocopy music.

* The Sopranos should only sing these bars if Altos and Men are absent.

All Saints

I heard a great voice

Text: Revelation 19: 1, 2; 21: 4; 19: 6
Music: Colin Mawby

© Copyright 1994 by Kevin Mayhew Ltd.
It is illegal to photocopy music.

* Sopranos may sing F# instead of A.

* Sopranos may sing F# instead of A.

PATRONAL FESTIVAL
How amiable are thy dwellings
Text: Psalm 84
Music: Colin Mawby

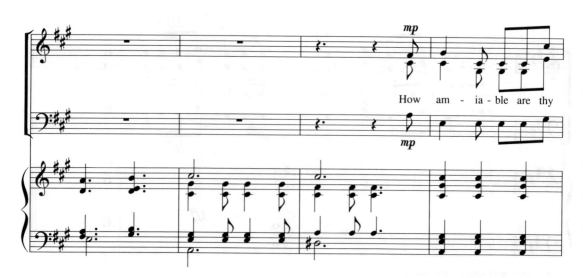

© Copyright 1994 by Kevin Mayhew Ltd.
It is illegal to photocopy music.